Here, There, Everywhere:
A Young Military Life

MARIANNE KELSEY ORESTIS

BASTILLE DAY 2021

authorHOUSE®

AuthorHouse™
1663 Liberty Drive
Bloomington, IN 47403
www.authorhouse.com
Phone: 833-262-8899

Published by AuthorHouse 10/27/2021

ISBN: 978-1-6655-4040-7 (sc)
ISBN: 978-1-6655-4039-1 (e)

Editor: Denise Moore

Works by Marianne Kelsey Orestis

SD Kelsey Collection, Northeast Historic
Film, Bucksport, Maine, 2009
My Brother Stevie: A Marine's Untold Story, Vietnam 1967, 2014
Here, There, Everywhere: A Young Military Life, Bastille Day 2021

Military Technical Advisor:
Specialist First Class Erik Garfield Enstrom
Military Police at Abu Ghraib Prison, Iraq
Rest in Peace and Love
February 26, 1989 - Monday, May 7, 2018

Foreword

I have written this memoir of a gypsy life to write down my stories of life in the West, the South, New England, Washington DC, and Europe so that my grandchildren and theirs will know. I kept no journals, so I have searched deep into my memory to remember things from so long ago. I used meditation and my editor's questions to refresh my memory. I also am a great fan of Wikipedia where I did quite a bit of research. They never let me down.

I wish to thank my editor, Denise Moore, Past Regent Topsham-Brunswick Chapter Maine State DAR, Topsham-Brunswick Chapter Librarian, and Maine State DAR Chaplain. DAR stands for the Daughters of the American Revolution, an organization I am very proud to belong to. I came to the DAR through my Southern Grandmother, Novella Bart Downing Kelsey. At her death, I inherited all her genealogy research and her love for Jesus. She left both with an abundance of heart.

Since my mother, there has been a trait of writing in my family. My oldest son, Christos III, has written four books. My grandson, Theodore Rex, is a talented descriptive writer. My daughter, Kelsey

Anne, wrote groundbreaking papers in college. My mother, Eileen Fee, wrote non-stop short stories and her major work, <u>Life's Great on the Queen,</u> is an epic poem. Her wish was to be published, but she did not live to see this realized. My youngest grandson, Birch, is always asking for or telling stories. Service is another family trait.

My father, Jack Kelsey, was a career 32-year military officer. My oldest grandson, Christos IV, is a natural leader. I had a career in mental health and founded Common Ties Mental Health Services. Grandsons Max and Straughan are focused on their respective paths, the sea and football. My son, Stephanos, is in service as a civilian foreign-service officer. His daughters, Selma, Sophia, and Eleanor, are all strong independent feminists, traits learned living around the world. They were in Cairo, Egypt, during the Arab Spring Revolution. They were in Rio de Janeiro at the start of the World Pandemic and now they are living in Bangladesh. They help to develop emerging nations.

We are all watched over by our guardian, Lt. Straughan Downing Kelsey, Jr., my brother, their uncle. He rests on a hill, under a shade tree in Arlington Cemetery. He is missed but his Spirit lives on in his nieces and nephews.

There is a price for freedom. We must remember.

Contents

For my children and those who follow

Two Very Important Things
1948

We left West Point, New York, in May of 1948, and climbed into our brand-new black Buick two-door car and proceeded to drive through the Midwest and the West, straight through the big state of Texas all the way to Albuquerque, New Mexico, where we were going to live at Clovis Airfield.

The land and the air of New Mexico were a complete opposite of Massachusetts and New York. Where those two states were lush and green with trees and flowering bushes and gardens, Albuquerque was a desert with red dirt and cacti. We moved into a small white square house with a backyard that was devoid of anything but dirt and cacti. We planted a vegetable garden, as there were lots of flowers on the cacti. I remember because I picked the flowers and then got adhesive tape on my hands to pull out the barbs. The garden was one of two events to stick in my mind. The second event came in August.

New Mexico is very dry with few storms. One day a large thunderstorm came through. It was an incredibly angry storm, and it grew very dark. And then, the hail came. My father was stationed at Clovis Airfield. After the storm we all went to the strip to see about the planes, as there was no hangar to store them in. They were fighter planes, Marauders. They had bombs and machine gun turrets. The airfield was a fighter base. After the storm, we went to see the planes and they were all banged up. They lost their squadron. As the planes had been badly dented, the airflow configurations of the Marauders were destroyed, and they could not be flown anymore.

This was also the time of the atom bomb and my father was somewhat involved. Details of that duty were never disclosed.

My parents were friendly with a military family in Albuquerque. It was a young family; the husband had been shot down and lost a leg and was a prisoner of war with the Germans. He was my father's best friend. We would all go to the rodeos together. They had longhorn steers and riding bronco bulls, and there were the young boys lassoing calves. Girls on quarter horses rode in dance with flying flags. Western gear was the order of the day, and all the males had on chaps. It was a cheerful colorful place.

In August, the State Fair came and as Albuquerque was the capital of New Mexico, it was a big fair; people coming and going, all in western clothes with cowboy hats and fringed chaps. There were rides and games and a shooting gallery. We enjoyed the rides and my brother, Stevie, did some shooting. He would become an expert marksman with the USMC. He would be killed in action in 1967 in Vietnam. He is a hero.

There were two things that stuck in my mind and one of them happened at the fair. We were at the games. We played many, but the penny toss stayed with us. The prize was a chick. Stevie played once – no win. He tried again. No win. He was very stubborn and determined, so he would not give up. He tossed and the penny dropped onto the platter. He had won. I can see him now, jumping up and down in excitement. The game man handed him a cardboard box with a lid and inside was his chick. And it peeped. My brother's five-year-old heart was flooded with love for this little, peeping chick. As far as he was concerned the Fair was over. He had to make a home for his chick.

We hurried back to our small white square home. In the home were a living room, kitchen, counter, and two bedrooms. There was also a furnace room. Our father told Stevie to put the chick in the furnace room as it gets cold at night in the desert and the chick needed the warmth of the furnace. My brother got towels and a pillow for himself. He was going to sleep with the chick. Our father said to Stevie to leave him in the box overnight and a proper home would be built the next day.

So, Stevie took his pillow and his blanket and made a bed for himself on the floor, right next to the chick. The chick was left in its box with the lid partly closed. During the dark and long chilly night, the chick died. The chick was discovered by my brother. He was devastated. This was his first pet, and he had given his heart to it. Never again would he love a pet, not even Pierre, a dog we had, but much later. This event stuck in my mind and in my heart.

As I was saying, it was August. The vegetable garden we had planted in June did not do very well because of the soil and water. However, the carrots grew.

My mother wanted to cook a stew. She needed carrots. All three of us, father, Stevie and me, went to pull carrots up for the stew. The earth was very dry. The soil was cracked it was so dry. I tried to pull up a carrot but could not. Stevie tried to pull up a carrot but could not. So, the three of us, from shortest to tallest, got in a line behind the carrot and took hold of its top and pulled. Nothing. We tried again. Nothing. The other carrots, I remember three, came out of the soil. But this carrot was a monster, so we were beginning to think. In unison, with great heave-hoes, we pulled again all together. The carrot that we dislodged from the garden was huge. Our father got a ruler to measure across the big carrot. It must have been 6" or the size of a saucer across the top. We all fell on our behinds. I remember the stew being extra tasty. It was an extremely unified family happy moment and I have remembered and treasured this memory all my life. And those are the events I remember in Albuquerque.

Then, with the squadron lost to the hailstorm, we moved to Montgomery, Alabama. Our father was going to the War College in Montgomery.

Jennymae

———— ❦ ————

We arrived in a segregated South in 1949. Segregation was the law of the South. I did not understand.

We settled in a rundown old Southern home with peeling wallpaper on my bedroom wall. We had moved into Fairfield, Alabama, which is near Montgomery. We were waiting for base housing.

I was enrolled at a kindergarten that was reached by walking through a college campus with large oak trees. There were flying squirrels in high numbers, and they would fly from tree branch to tree branch. Many did not make the flight, and we would walk around the corpses of the squirrels on the way to school. The school had a swing set, and I remember my mother and I swinging on the swings with our long hair flowing. We were wearing matching lilac floral dresses with purple ribbons. We were both incredibly happy. Mother was a beautiful woman with long curly hair. She was from Brooklyn Heights, New York. She was a professional model appearing in catalogues, Life Magazine, and runways. She was a graduate of the New York Professional Children's School. It was in

Alabama that she cut her hair short and lost her curls. My school did not work out, as they did not have a thorough inventory of tools to teach, so I went to the bigger public school across the street. The street was a major two-lane thoroughfare.

At this school, I started to hate school. That hate went through all 12 grades. I struggled with undiagnosed dyslexia. I had attended 13 grammar schools and three high schools by the time I graduated in 1963 in Ohio. I am a self-taught learner and I get my continuing education from the books I read and remember. History is my favorite subject, especially European history.

While we lived in this house, I would walk across the street to school and the dog we had would wait for me. His name was Joe. He was a loving, medium-sized shorthaired black mutt. He was very smart. One day, as the school year went on, I was trying to cross the street to get home and Joe was on the other side of the street. He ran into the street to come to me because I needed help, and he knew it. A car ran into him, and he died right in front of my eyes in the middle of the street. My father was there, and my brother came out, and we all cried mightily. We all loved Joe. We buried him in a farmer's field in the country. We would not have another dog until we were in Virginia in 1955. Joe's death left a large hole in my heart.

In Fairfield, we had a gentleman neighbor. He was a kind man with a twinkle in his eye. He was a gardener. He had a large, beautiful garden that neighbored our back yard. It was very peaceful in the backyard due to his gaily-colored garden. We played archery and cowboys and Indians. Stevie had chaps from New Mexico and western clothes. He looked the part of the cowboy. I was always the Indian. One night we were walking through our arbor to the back door when we saw a huge spider web blocking the path to the door. It was gigantic and the black spider was nothing to mess with. He became our pet. We fed him flies and moths and made sure his web stayed intact. We took care of him until we finally got into base housing at Maxwell Air Force Base in the officers' quarters. Stevie got his first scar. It was on his head. He received the scar on the side of his head shooting bow and arrow. An arrow whisked his head. All his life you could see it.

It was at this time that mother became pregnant with our sister Lisa. She needed help, what with the stifling heat and humidity. Base housing was basic. Our quarters were spacious with two bedrooms, living room, dining area, and screened porch. This is when Jennymae came to our lives. Jennymae was an integral part of our lives and she was with us for two years. She helped mother through her pregnancy and birth of Lisa.

Jennymae was part of an army of Alabamian maids that worked for white people. She was professional and kind. She always wore a white uniform and white nurse's shoes. She did anything my mother said and did it well. She was proud of her work and efforts and could not be trifled with. She treated us with greatest of respect and expected respect back. She cooked, she cleaned, and she took care of Stevie and me. The home hummed.

Being with Jennymae was a comforting feeling. She was a perfectionist in her work, and everything sparkled. She was also kind and huggable. She lived under a stressful burden and never once said a word about her life. It was just father and mother, Stevie, Marianne, and Lisa. Then, it was time to leave, so Jennymae came to help with the packing and the new baby. Something happened between her and my mother, I do not know what. Jennymae was fired. It was a very loud separation, and it has stayed with me to this day. Just as had segregation.

I did not know races or disharmony and unquiet until Alabama. It was all over my knowledge and experience level. I was 6. But I noticed it. At the train station in Montgomery, I saw lots of black people in separate areas. I saw lots of white people in separate areas. It was disquieting to me. I had to go the restroom, so I saw a sign that showed a bathroom, so I went in alone. I discovered I was the first person to integrate a restroom in the South. It was a colored restroom. The colored restroom was clean and white. It had a bank of white sinks on one wall. It had a section of whitewashed stalls. The walls were white. There is no recording of this or proof, but it happened in 1951.

Segregation and injustice have stayed with me to this day. I am pleased to have witnessed the struggles in Selma, Alabama, to get the Voting Rights Act passed in 1965 under President Lyndon Johnson. People were beaten, skulls fractured, arrests made just because black people wanted to vote and eat in white areas. As we were transferred to places in the South it seemed as if we had arrived just before the protests. I followed Martin Luther King, Jr. in the press and television as he went from city to city making slow but deliberate progress. There was great enmity from the whites of the South. I am a product of the struggle.

Not only did I witness the clashes, read about the clashes, and absorb the clashes, I was a participant in August of 1963 in Washington, DC in the "I Have A Dream" moment with Mahalia Jackson, Martin Luther King, and John Lewis. John Lewis was a Lieutenant in Dr. King's army at that time. I saw them all on the steps of the Lincoln Memorial, and I saw the federal troops blocking access to the Lincoln Memorial during Black Lives Matter protests in DC In June-July of 2020. So, Jennymae has been fighting for equality since 1951, when she was taking care of white people.

The Korean War broke out. We were originally supposed to go to Taegu Air Base Korea, a fighter jet plane base, but because of the war, Daddy went to Taegu Air Base alone and we, the four of us, went to Lake Worth, Florida.

I do not remember feeling much of anything about the upcoming separation. I was heartbroken, as I had become Daddy's girl, but this is military life, and it was the new reality. Nothing could be done to change the facts, so one just moved on.

The Veterinarian

$\textcircled{v}$

It was 1630. The Winthrop Fleet set sail from England to Plymouth Colony, Massachusetts. The fleet consisted of 10 ships and William Kelsey was on one. William Kelsey was age 30. When the fleet arrived in Massachusetts, North America, William went to the bustling port of Boston. He stayed there long enough to find a wife. Her name was Tabitha. They would have 13 children. A family was born. William and Tabitha settled on farm acreage in Cambridge, Massachusetts. After a time and at the beginning of the Great Migration, William and Tabitha moved to what was called Hartford, Connecticut, and then on to Ohio.

The Great Migration was the diaspora of the Winthrop and Mayflower pilgrims to new areas of America. They were farmers. What the Kelsey's truly were - they were soldiers. The military has been with the family ever since. A Kelsey has been in each war, clash, and skirmish since then. A descendant of theirs, their 7th generation great-grandson was named Harry Ray Kelsey. He was my grandfather. He was a soldier.

He held officer rank. He was a veterinarian in the Calvary. He was born in Ohio in 1879 and traveled to Burgess, Virginia, which is tidewater country. This area of the state is lowland wet area and was quite rural back in the day. During the colonial times it was home to Revolutionaries and the temperament of Burgess was hard working and military. Two prominent families of the 1800's were families by the names of Downing and Blackwell. The Blackwell's had blonde, almost white, hair. That trait has been passed down. Captain Samuel Blackwell, Jr. is my Daughters of the American Revolution ancestor. Over time the Downing's and Blackwell's became Downing and Kelsey. Downing's have sat in Congress, served in positions of authority in the government and in soldiering.

Harry Ray Kelsey traveled to Burgess, set up shop, saw and began courting Novella Bart Downing. Bart was born in Burgess, Virginia, in 1889. She grew up to be a genteel Southern woman and she was very beautiful. She and Kels had three children, born in tidewater Newport News, Virginia, near Salters Creek. The first son was born in 1915, my father in 1917, and the third child, a girl, was born in 1921. Bart was the softness in the family and raised up her children in the Baptist tradition. To his dying day, my father prayed every day. Bart was exceptional with embroidery and cross-stitch, and I have her work hanging in my home. I inherited her skill with her hands as I crochet. Bart loved family history, and I have all her records, photos and memorabilia. She brought tenderness, talents, belief in Jesus, and tradition to our family. During World War II, she died of kidney cancer, a disease that could be cured today. That was in 1943. My father has a deep hatred of the American Red Cross because they did not let him know about his mother until he was out of the war theater. Kels remained a widower until 1952 when he married his second wife, a Southern Virginian genteel woman, Irene.

Kels was military and served in the Spanish American War under Teddy Roosevelt as his Commanding Officer and World War I. He served with the Calvary during both wars; he served with distinction. In World War I, he was put in charge of the mules going to Europe. The Europeans needed mules in the hundreds daily as the British, at the beginning of the war had 80 motor vehicles. Mules would become the workhorse of the effort, pulling cannons, supplies, and people to and fro. The food requirements for the mules were so great and in such short supply they were often fed sawdust cakes. Even with that diet, the mules exhibited stamina, endurance, and strength. It was Kels' job to get them there.

Kels' job was to find mules, mostly in Texas and the South. As the war went on mules were obtained from other countries also. But Kels had to corral and categorize the inventory of mules and get them on the transport ships to Europe. I am sure he went overseas on those ships also making sure the mules arrived useable for war. At the end of the war, over 2 million horses had been killed, abandoned, wounded, and shot. The number of mules remains unknown, but one number that emerged is 1 million. I first met him when I was 7.

Korea

It was the gathering of the clan in Lake Worth, Florida. My mother and the children arrived in 1950-1951. The two sets of grandparents arrived at the same time.

First came Marguerite and Jonathan Michael Fee, all the way from Brooklyn Heights, New York. Next came Harry Ray and Irene Kelsey from Newport News, Virginia. They all moved to us to help during this time of war and separation.

Marguerite was the apple of his eye, my grandfather. They bought a new home and painted it pink, inside and out. Pink walls, pink carpet, pink furniture. Pink was my grandmother's favorite color. At first there was no lawn. It was all sand and sand spurs, nasty hurtful sticky weeds. They lived there the rest of their lives. They built a beautiful lawn and Florida garden.

Kels and Irene bought an old Southern property with low roof and screened porches, perfect for hurricane season. There was also a large garage with an apartment above that was used for friends and family. The floors were all cedar planks. They lived there the rest of their lives. When Kels was 92 he climbed a coconut tree to get a coconut but fell. He landed on his head and died a few days later. My father, when he was 82 was climbing a stepladder to reach the top of the parrot's cage to cover it for the night, and he slipped and landed on his head and died a week later.

Mother moved into a new home that was at the end of the paved road with sand dunes and sandspurs and coconut trees which was all one could see. Many years later, I went back to that house and it looked like it was almost in the middle of Lake Worth. Lake Worth was just beginning to boom in 1951. The house had no grass, so we planted Saint Augustine grass. We did not know it had taken and grown until Daddy came home from Korea and cut the lawn. Before it was all sandspurs and weeds. Each time we moved we took our furnishings. When I saw the two pink love seats in the living room, I knew this was home. The Catholic school was a half-mile down the road. Stevie was an excellent student and became an altar boy. I made my First Communion at this school and church.

We had gone to Lake Worth Beach that morning of First Communion. The ocean was rough, and I went into my waist, just body surfing. I was a strong swimmer. The Lake Worth Beach was wide and flat with no stones or boulders offshore, so it was good for playing in. That day I must have been stung by a jellyfish. It was May, and that is the season for them. After spending the morning playing on the beach and in the surf, we went home to prepare for the church service. By the time I was at the head of the aisle of the church, I was all swollen up and bright red. My mother was aghast. I made my communion and went home to recover but I looked like a ripe watermelon. I am allergic to jellyfish.

While my father was off, fighting the war, there were two families that stayed close to us: the Steelie's and the Murphy's. They had three children each, just like us. The Steelie's were military and the Murphy's were civilian. They were friends with my mother. I was friends with Mrs. Sandwich who lived in the yard behind us. She was an elderly woman living alone, a Floridian all her life. I remember going to her home and she would make me sandwiches and we would talk. Mrs. Sandwich was not her real name; it was what I called her. There was also, over many sand dunes, a diner where the owner took a personal interest in my welfare. I can recall eating foot-long hot dogs with mustard and pickle relish with him in his restaurant and him shooting the breeze. It was always an adventure to go to his diner. I also began taking gymnastics, which I practiced until my last cartwheel in 2004. It was a one-handed cartwheel, and I am afraid I handicapped my left hand. To this day it is bothersome, and I do not know what is wrong with it.

Next door, in Lake Worth, lived a young family, and they had a TV. Everyday at 4, we would go over to the house to watch Howdy Doody. It was the highlight of my day everyday. They were beginning a hardware and paint store in Lake Worth. When I returned many years later, it was a major Lake Worth establishment.

Also, many years later, I found my father's correspondence from Korea, so I now have an idea of the war and life as a Commanding Officer. It was during Korea that he was promoted to full Colonel.

The year is 1951-52. At Taegu Air Base, Colonel SD Kelsey was Commanding Officer. The base was located on the Pacific Ocean in the southern part of the Korean countryside. Jets and bombers flew from there. There was an Officer's Club, German Shepherd guard dog training sites, flying fields, practice bombing sites, and recreation parks. During his tour of duty, Marilyn Monroe came with the USO. A photo was taken of the two of them and, many years later, after they had died, the photo was displayed on the jumbotron at Times Square, New York.

Koreans were horrifically displaced during the war. Their infrastructure was gone, having been bombed out. Irrigation of growing fields was accomplished by paddle wheels manually operated by a Korean farmer walking in place on the wheel. Many others carried needed water on their shoulders using two buckets held by a pole on their shoulders.

Banners were seen saying, in English, "GIVE US UNIFICATION OR DEATH." Crops were harvested as best they could grow them in this difficult time, but people have needs: food, shelter, water and these needs do not stop in war. Ladies swept the dust of war with straw brooms, making more dust than it picked up. Through it all they smiled for they were free. Many decades later my son Christos III married Grace Hahm, a Korean American. Her father Reverend S.K. Michael Hahm was a teenager during the war, and he was from a village in the North. He and 7 friends hid in a cave during some heavy fighting between North Koreans and Marines. The Marines found them and told them to run and to run fast. They went with the Marines to the South. They never saw their families again. In the early 2000s, he and his friends were instrumental in working with the North Korean and South Korean governments to reopen the border at the Demilitarized Zone so that relatives could visit for the first time since 1952.

The weather was harsh, the terrain cruel, and almost as many American soldiers were killed during this war as in Vietnam 20 years later.

While in Korea, Dad had a dream of breaking the sound barrier. He flew his jet high into the sky, as high as the jet would go and then turned his plane into a nosedive and screeched downward. He leveled off at 2,000 feet. He had not accomplished his goal. He never did.

He arrived back in Florida in 1952 having been a passenger on a Military Air Transport plane and he was wearing his flight suit and carrying a Korean bow and arrow. He was devil-may-care. But he was home. In World War II, he was a bomber pilot stationed in England dropping bombs on Germany. He tells the tale of a flight:

I graduated from AT-6 school, Sacramento, in July 1942, and was assigned 21ˢᵗ Bomb Group, (B-26). Mac Dill Field. Joined 323ʳᵈ Bomber. I joined a group cadre a few days later, 453 Bomb Squadron. I became qualified as first pilot with 12 hours B-26 time and IP a couple of hours later. Colonel Jim Adducci and I flew together a lot. Most notable flight was Mac Dill to Langley when 18-year-old Engineer-gunner S/Sgt Bill Crowe asked me whether the generator switches should be on or off; we decided that "off" seemed to be the right way. Shortly afterward, Lt. Saul Rubin, Navigator, remarked that it was too dark to pick out ground features and his instruments were acting up. Lights began flickering and the propellers (props) began increasing and decreasing pitch, making an ungodly racket. After several minutes spent in searchlight beams at Charleston as a possible navigation destination, we landed at Savannah with no electricity in the aircraft and all airport lights blacked out. Being arrested at that time, was a picnic compared to the withering scorn next day when M/Sgt Pappy Greenwood, Squadron Chief arrived to bail us out.

October 1942 saw us at Myrtle Beach, South Carolina—the first full group assigned there—where we trained until early 1943. Every B-26 man will pause in quiet humility and love before the memory of our fellow crews who crashed and died there in those months so we survivors could learn our trade.

A crash landing was one of the times we were being trained at Myrtle Beach. One wheel fell off on take-off, and we slid in beside the runway. The aircraft rotated slightly as it slid along and moved down the runway at a 5-10-degree angle to the axis. Unfortunately, a crash truck was heading in the opposite direction and never turned aside, drove through our still running engine. I believe that six civilian firemen were killed. May God rest their souls, they were Marauder (B-26) men too. Amazingly, Captain Dick Travis, my good friend for 6-years and my Squadron Commander, was riding the crash truck and passed between the turning propellers and the fuselage with minor scratches. I will never forget the scene. Inside the aircraft the sharp impact had injured S/Sgt Bill Crower's back, but he kept flying for many more years until this and several other accidents, plus being shot down over France and walking out via Spain, eventually grounded him.

I believe it was April 6, 1943, when we received B-26C's stripped – no co-pilot or radio operator – horrible airplanes at Baer Field, Fort Wayne, Indiana, and flew the southern route to the United Kingdom. I recall men at Atkinson Field, British Guiana, trying to sell us huge amethyst, topaz, aquamarines, citrines for a nickel apiece. Then, via Ascension, we landed in Liberia, Dakar, Marrakesh.

Our Squadron was temporarily on the 322ⁿᵈ Groups base when we flew those two disastrous low-level missions to the Phillips Factory in Amsterdam. Soon thereafter, when the other three 323ʳᵈ Group Squadrons joined us, we moved to Earle's Cologne.

Between the summer of 1943 and spring 1945, when I was transferred to 387 Bomber Group, I served under Major to Colonel General Sam Anderson during this time and again in Korea when he had been promoted to Lieutenant General and I'd like to pay him this tribute: He's probably the smartest, most considerate general I've ever known. Completely mission-oriented, he takes care of his troops. West Point and United States Air Force can be proud of him.

I believe it was April 1945 when I was transferred to 387ᵗʰ Bomber Group AS Group Operations under Colonel Grover Brown. He is another of the very best officers the USAF produced – a real leader. Almost immediately after, Colonel Brown went home, and Colonel Phil Sykes took over. I became deputy and we moved to Beck, Holland for the next month or so, still with airplanes.

Then we moved back to France – town of Meharicourt, and somehow, Montes-Gassicourt sticks in my mind and so does Rosieres-en- Santence. First, they took our airplanes to Germany and cut them into little pieces, including two aircrafts, which had flown the Atlantic and had something like 130 and 140 missions without an abort. So, we had lots of formations and reviews, we sent ¼ of each squadron to Paris each week on 7-day passes, we did lots of housekeeping, and we set up Tiger Stripe

University. Finally, they took our vehicles and equipment and then they sent the group home for use in the Pacific, except me. As a regular Army type, I was not allowed to go home and was reassigned as Wing A-4 until they went home and to the 144th Group and, finally, in December, I went home on 14-days leave and never went back.

On one of the last flights before losing our aircraft, I flew as IP with a new replacement, and we were descending at about 7,000 feet and intending to penetrate slightly the edge of a small thunderstorm near Saint Quentin. I have never experienced such a thunderstorm!!!

As soon as we entered, the nose was shattered by a baseball size hailstone which wounded the bombardier and knocked him back up the tunnel, a second one splintered my windshield (amazingly it did not shatter inside the cockpit and the aircraft assumed a nose high, 115-degree right roll position. In recovering from this, I caused the whole crew to get vertigo and tumbled the gyros. Flying entirely on needle, ball and airspeed, I managed to exit the cloud slightly nose-down in a 10-degree bank. The storm had closed two of three of our operational fields, and, so, we finally found an empty field (Roye'Amy) and landed at a stall speed of 145mph. The plane never flew again.

The Pentagon

———— ✺ ————

D evil-may-care and safe at home. Soon after his return, we were stationed to the Pentagon in the Washington, DC megalopolis; at the time, it was not a megalopolis.

We drove to Fairfax County, Virginia. It was located near what would be the DC, Maryland, Virginia beltway, a superhighway that encircled DC. At that time, 1952, Fairfax County was all horse and farmland, but for sale signs were up all over, and the area was just beginning to transform into the megalopolis.

We settled in an old Virginia home in a wooded area. The area was called Sleepy Hollow. The house had a two-car detached garage and a wraparound porch. It was a large house with a finished basement which we used for parties and watching TV. We got our first television when the Mickey Mouse Club first started. There was another first at Sleepy Hollow – Pierre joined our family.

Pierre was a puppy. He was a royal standard chocolate brown poodle. He was a perfect dog as he was smart, easy to train. Loving and loyal. Years later, in Paris, France, the French would see him out for a promenade and call out, "Bonjour, Il est La Grande Caniche."

They loved him. He was so magnificent. He died in Florida, after living in many homes and across the sea, at the age of 20.

We lived in Sleepy Hollow for a year and then moved to Arlington County in a new community that was called Lake Barcroft, as the new homes being built were centered around the lake. There were many swimming meets in that lake and enjoyable times held on the shore. We did not get a boat.

The home we moved into was newly built. It was a three-story, three-bedroom home with white paint on the exterior and hot pink shutters and front door. We added a picket fence for Pierre in the backyard. Behind our property were woods. Across the street and up a bit was Bailey's Crossroads school where I attended. I enjoyed that school and was a school patrolman. I took art classes and won first prize in an art show. My painting was of a quarter horse on a lake, but it was done in Grandma Moses style. I became a celebrity for a brief time. I also took dance classes, ballroom dancing. President Kennedy's press secretary lived nearby. His name was Pierre Salinger. But the big draw for this time was the Pentagon.

My father was working inside the Pentagon. I do not know what he did, but, in a later station, he was head of Intelligence, so I think it had to do with that. Weekends were special and the Pentagon made it so.

On one weekend a month I would go with my father to the Pentagon to use the indoor gym. The gym was in the basement of this building. It was large, expansive, and well-lit. There were trampoline mats in the floor with support mats all around. It was very safe. I would do gymnastics on these trampolines and had a wonderful time. As I recall this area of the gym was not busy, and I had the place to myself.

After working out, we would go into hallways of the Pentagon to go to a snack bar to get hamburgers and a vanilla milkshake. The hallways were an adventure unto themselves: dark, windowless, and fantasy. The walls of the hallways were lined with shops from all over the world. The only lighting was the neon lights of the shops and the white lights inside the stores. It was like Christmas lighting and it was beautiful. The walls of the hallway were black so all you could see were the colorful lights and they appeared to twinkle. We would exit the building into the sun of the day and the sun was so bright it hurt my eyes.

We also and had many visitors to Lake Barcroft. The extended family came, so I met cousins and aunts and uncles. We would take them to the memorials in DC. The memorials are for all the American people, and they are beautiful. Shimmering in white granite and marble and oversized sculptures and grandeur. My very favorite is the Jefferson Memorial at cherry blossom time.

We would also take our guests to Great Falls Park in Virginia, which borders the Chesapeake Canals in Georgetown in Washington. Both are scenic walks, and the park has a carousel with organ music and a bunch of brass rings that you would try to grab as you went around and around so that you could get another ride, and it would be free. Great Falls Park was a state park and, as in its name, there were streams and a narrow river that flowed over large boulders and made beautiful waterfalls. We would climb on the boulders and put our feet in the falls. Years later, I attended college in Arlington, Virginia, and would still go the Great Falls Park. I think I left a piece of my heart there.

We also went into DC every other Saturday to be on television. It was the era of bobby socks and skinny ties. Young men wore white sports coats and short hair or crew cuts. Young women wore ponytails and full skirts, especially the poodle skirt. My brother and I were regulars on a precursor to the American Bandstand. It was called the Milt Grant Record Hop. It was the original and when American Bandstand aired, they were matching competitors. It ran until 1961. We were on in 1957-58. Steve and I rode the elevator after one show with only one other passenger – Johnny Mathis. I did not get his autograph but years later while I was having brunch with the Rolling Stones, I got Mick Jagger's autograph. It was 1972.

My husband and I went to an Italian wedding in New Jersey. It was memorable. We stayed in the City at the Plaza Hotel. At 2:45 p.m., we went down to the Plaza dining room for brunch. My husband ordered eggs benedict. By this time, it was 3 p.m., and there were maybe two other tables full of diners. The dining room was empty but for the three tables. The server told my husband that eggs benedict was not served after 3 p.m. My husband was quite upset at this but ordered another brunch item. At this time there was a commotion at the entrance to the restaurant and servers appeared from out of the woodwork. I noticed and looked at the large group entering. There was only one reason hippies with money could eat at the Plaza. They were the Rolling Stones. Jade Jagger was on the hand of Mick Jagger. The whole group was there. To say I was thrilled is putting it mildly. They sat at a banquette near to us. They were so close I could hear the conversation with the numerous servers. They ordered eggs benedict. It was 3:30PM. Instead of saying they did not serve eggs benedict after 3 p.m., the servers said that their order would be right out. My husband was furious. I was excited. The Stones were happy. Shortly, a server approached their group with a business card from one of the three full tables in the room. He asked for an autograph for the people at the other table. The request was granted, and the server withdrew with the business card. My husband's face was buried down by the tabletop, he was so angry. I asked him if he had a business card on him and he said yes. I took the card. I got up and walked right over to the banquette and introduced myself and said I was a fan. I was also 8 months pregnant with my daughter. Mick spoke right up. Jade did not look so happy. She is indeed very beautiful. Mick and I had a 10-minute conversation about spoiling boys versus girls. This was before ultrasound. I had said I would spoil a girl and Mick got upset that I would not spoil a boy also. At the resolution of the brief argument, I presented the business card and Mick Jagger signed it with love. I then, touched Keith Richards on the shoulder, ever so gently, and departed the banquette for my own table. My husband never got eggs benedict. We departed the restaurant, and my feet did not touch the ground for the rest of the day.

It was at Lake Barcroft that my sister started school. She went each morning in a taxicab. She proved to be a good student. Steve attended a Catholic school and from here, he did so very well, that he got a scholarship to a private school in New Hampshire. The family felt that he was so very bright, with an IQ of 160 – same as DaVinci – that he needed the intense and highly regarded education at Saint Paul's Preparatory School located in New England.

We had never been to New England and I remember the drive we took in the pink Chevy station wagon to get him there. We took main roads, as I-95 was not yet built and highways were not in existence-just roads, which today we would call country roads. We saw the woods lining the roads with their leaves turning into a chorus of color. I do not really recall any cities, just the roads.

The station wagon was loaded with my brother's belongings. He was to board for 4 years. At that time, we did not know we were going to Paris, France. The future was unclear, but Steve was settled into a time of study and reflection. He met his wife at a dance at this school. They dated all through high school and college and got married shortly after their final graduation. He was dead 7 months later.

With my brother safe and challenged in school, life went on in DC. I finished 7th grade, and at my ceremony, I learned we were moving to France. I was told that Steve would remain in New Hampshire and we would be moving in a few weeks. We put the house on the market, packed up, and went to New York City to stay at Governor's Island in the New York Harbor while we awaited our ship. I do not remember if you could see the Statue of Liberty from the island.

It was toward the end of May 1958. My 13th birthday was approaching. We sailed on the USS America for Le Havre, France. We traveled by train to Paris. May 22nd I was standing at the Arc de Triomphe, and it was my thirteenth birthday. A new world had arrived.

Paris

I found myself standing at the Arc de Triomphe on my 13th birthday. And I marveled. We were staying at a hotel on the Champs Elysée just across the lane. We had a view of the Champs Elysée from the 3rd floor. There was an old fashioned elevator from the 1920's in the center of the whole building, it took us from our floor to the rez-de-chausse, which was the main floor or ground floor. In Europe, the next floor up would be the first floor. The entry and lobby were open to each other. There were pots of palms and richly upholstered chairs. The desk was high and of a polished darker wood. Not far from there, the Chinese restaurant dining room served from early morning till late at night. The lighting was low and the space dark except for the front doors, where an inviting light streamed beckoning one to walk through and step onto the greatest boulevard I had very seen.

I went out on to the sidewalk and decided to walk up the boulevard towards the Arc de Triomphe. I crossed the circle and stood at the Tomb of the Unknown soldier. I looked down the length of the Champs Elysée from its center. I saw broad sidewalks lined with lovingly tendered chestnut trees. On the sidewalks were many people of all races and colors strolling, sitting at café's, painting oils, vendors with carts, and the metro entrances. The Metro (subway) entrances are works of art that distinguish the great boulevard from all the others.

We went to a sidewalk café. We sat outside on little round tables with iron trim and I, for the first time, began to absorb the language. It is truly an elegant way to communicate. I learned my first French at that time: bifteck frites.

I must expand on the chestnut trees lining the Champs Elysée. The magnificence of all of them so precisely positioned equal distant from each other and across from each other was just breath- taking. The beauty of a chestnut tree and the glory of all of them in spring bloom has left a lasting image on my mind. Indeed, I have found a variety of chestnut tree in Maine, and I will be buried under its protection. In Paris, the trees were saved, and they are a national treasure and given care accordingly. In the late fall, the chestnut nuts fall to the ground and then the vendors gather them all up roast them in their cast iron skillets and fires and sell them in newspaper wrapped cones for Parisians to enjoy for which they have looked forward to all season.

We stayed on the Champs Elysée a few days and then moved to our new French home in a Parisian suburb called Le Vesinet. Le Vesinet was a bedroom community with shopping, a large community park, a farmer's market, and a flower market. It had a train station, as trains are one of the chief means of transportation. Scooters and motorcycles were also common. By being in Paris with all the chestnut trees, gardens, sidewalk café's, flower stands, and an entirely different ambience, and then being located in a posh suburb with its architecture, gardens, churches, and markets, I sensed that I was on the adventure of a lifetime. I became very observant. I remembered.

We moved into 60 Rue de Croissy. It was an old French home comprised of three floors, 5 bedrooms, dining room, library, and kitchen with a garden in the back yard and lawn and flowers in the front yard. It was enclosed by an eight-foot-high solid fence made from stone and painted plaster with tile on the top. The driveway and road were separated by an eight-foot-high double gate, which was carved and had curves on the top of it. All the homes had such fences. I remember that there was a small gothic church or chapel nearby, and it is in that church that I spoke my first French sentence, which was to ask a lady what time it was. Quelle heure est-il?

A 250-cc motorcycle on the house's property became my chief form of transportation. The motorcycle was equipped with basket and saddlebags, so it was used as a major way to get from point 'a' to point 'b'. This was all happening 15-years after the Nazi occupation. Paris and Europe were just beginning to recover from the darkest of times. People lived at marginal or somewhat better income levels. Transportation was mostly bicycling, electric bicycles, scooters, motorcycles, or very small cars (quatre-cheveau) that were like tin cans. For upper-class people, there were the cars called the Citroën. My father, the Colonel, bought a Peugeot and went from Le Vesinet to Fontainebleau, which is a long distance and across many areas of Cypress trees and empty spaces so as to allow funnels for strong wind and such was the case with him for; he was blown off the road down an embankment and broke his collarbone.

But that happened later than May, it was in spring. This was June and the flowers, which were all over, and the trees were in full bloom and it was spectacular. In France, Independence Day is in July on the 14th. That also happens to be my brother's birthday. We were all together at the American Embassy with Ambassador Amory Houghton on that day, that day of Independence and birthday. And the complete splendor of the French Military and Resistance Fighters as led by President and Liberator Charles de Gaulle, and the fantasy concert and fireworks at Versailles' Gardens was thought to be for him who was 15. We gathered on the rooftop of the Embassy where there is a patio. Our view was beyond compare. Bastille Day holds great importance for me.

What I remember is the sea of red. The military dress uniform, as I recall, is a red jacket, French blue slacks with a red stripe down the outer-seam. There were sashes and sabers, and their hats had a plume. I believe the entire French military was there, it was a marvel to behold. President de Gaulle walked at the head of the procession. Their jets flew formation above with tendrils of red, white, and blue smoke. They were a glorious army; they were victors and they marched accordingly. The parade was so large it went on for hours. The weather was perfect. There was a military band with lots of brass, gold braids, and gusto. They played the Marseillaise, The French National Anthem. It was all very stirring. And then it wound down. Night was coming, so it was on to the next celebration: fireworks at Versailles.

It remains in my mind an impression of wonder. This was a light and music show that I only just glimpsed in the movie *Fantasia* and, now, here I was a spectator. It was held on La Grande Perspective facing the Grand Canal in Versailles. Latona's Fountain was just there. The fountain faces the other four fountains named for the seasons. It was lit up and water was gently splashing into the pond-like basin. The fountain was large and graceful. Seated to its side were the soldier musicians in their dress uniforms of the French Military orchestra. As the sky darkened, the fountain stopped and the orchestra began to play classical music. If I remember correctly it was Baroque. In the magnificence of the palace shimmering of light just over my shoulder and the gardens in front of me, the music playing ever so sweetly. It was all quite enchanting. Then the fireworks exploded in the sky. It was just overwhelmingly beautiful.

The Metamorphoses was written by Ovid. It is the story of the goddess Latona who is mother to Apollo and Diana, and they are all being tormented by the inhabitants of Lycia. Latona gets the god Jupiter to intervene and he obliges, turning the Lycians into frogs and lizards. Latona's Fountain is sculptured to tell that story. There are four more fountains and a grand canal. There is an orangery that is outdoors in late spring to fall and inside fall and winter. There are innumerable sculptured boxwoods with paths bordered by elegant Cypress trees. There was the Royal Way, the path the King and his court would take to enter and then to stroll through the garden, and all could be seen from the Hall of Mirrors inside Versailles

The American Embassy was located at the corners of the Champs Elysée and the Place de la Concorde. The square was near a meat market during the French Revolution. Plus, the guillotine was located at its center. The King and Queen were beheaded there, and there was such a stench of blood the animals would balk at being driven there. Now the obelisk of freedom stands at its center. From this spacious square one can go to the Seine, the Tuileries Garden, which faces the Louvre, or go back to the Champs Elysée. But why were we there?

My father, Colonel Jack Kelsey, was promoted and stationed to the Supreme Headquarters Allied Powers Europe (S.H.A.P.E.), which was found in the town of Versailles. It has been relocated to Brussels, which is why there have been several terrorist bombings in that city. At this time, John F. Kennedy was president, and he was to come to Paris with his wife, Jackie. During their visit, Jackie was a sensation, and it seemed as though the President was just along for the ride. There were many official presentations, speeches, and press opportunities. President Kennedy made a trip to S.H.A.P.E., and my father was introduced. He and my mother were invited to a governmental ball at Versailles. My mother had a gown made by a French seamstress and my father wore his Air Force dress blues. They looked quite the elegant pair. The ball was held in the Hall of Mirrors from which you could see the Latona's Fountain. Except for King Louis XIV's private quarters, the Hall of Mirrors, or Salon de Glace, was one of the most splendid of all the Palace. It must have seen to them to be magical. The President and Mrs. Kennedy were in attendance along with President General Charles de Gaulle. Both of my parents shook hands with President and Mrs. Kennedy and President General de Gaulle.

With all the excitement, time went by swiftly. It became time to think of education. After comparisons of the American school and French school, it was decided that an immersive education would be best. I was enrolled at a private Catholic boarding school called Marymount sur Seine a Neuilly. It was in Paris in the gardens of the Bois de Boulogne along the Seine. It quickly became my favorite school. I am not a good student but through their teaching and example I learned algebra, etiquette, and French. I became at home on the broad sidewalks of Paris and learned how to use the metro and the trains. The train station I used the most was Gare St Lazare. This rail hub, one of 6 Parisian hubs, was second busiest, with Gare du Nord being the busiest. I used it to get back and forth to Le Vesinet, and I spoke French to use it. It was not as common in Europe for Europeans to be fluent in English as it is now.

While a student at Marymount, I made good friends with Silvia Ospina, a boarder from Bogota, Columbia. We all went to the Jardin du Luxembourg and rode the children's train and walked through the beautiful children's gardens. We had a wonderful time, and Sylvia and I became close. She was in Paris for protection. Her father was a politician in Columbia and went on to become President. He was assassinated. I do not know what happened to Sylvia. She was 13. The assassination happened later.

The nuns who taught and cared for us were smart, nurturing, and strict. They are the Religious of the Sacred Heart of Mary. Their ministries include educational, pastoral, and social services. They have an elementary and high school in Manhattan and high schools and colleges across the globe. There founder was a French religious nun named Jean Gailhac, and the mother house was a chateau in Bezier, France, located in the middle of vineyards in wine country in Southern France. I traveled with a portion of the school to see it and to watch the most private ceremony of becoming apostolates and nuns. Unfortunately, I had the green death and could not stay for the whole ceremony. Water in Europe is not good, bottled water only.

At school, there were two-second floor buildings made from stone, plaster, and vines. One building was for the international borders and one for the Irish girls. They are a mystery to this day. We could not interact with them. They looked to be in high school. I do not know if they were training to be nuns or if they were just upper echelon girls getting a superb education. There was a chapel and a dining room and classrooms. It was all very elegant. There was an eight-foot-high stone fence along the street. I loved this school so much that I enrolled at Marymount College Virginia when I was 18.

With our stay in France, mostly everyday business there was not much happening during the school year. During the summer, this was different. My brother flew from Concord, New Hampshire, to Orly Airport, and we explored. The Paris airport is now known as

Charles De Gaulle Field. The International Airshow is held there annually.

My brother and I became flaneurs, strollers. Together, we explored the side streets of Paris, the flower markets, the book markets, the Marché Puce. The Marche Puce was my mother's favorite place. It is a gigantic consignment shop full of European antiques. She came home to Saint-Germain-en-Lay (we had moved) very excited after a visit there. She purchased copper pots, chairs, dishes, a metal painted tray and she made her best find – a large marble salon-de-bain tabletop, which I still have. It is beautiful. It is from the early 1800s. I have the metal painted tray. The souvenirs one collects have been lost over time. But what we saw together, I have placed in a very special compartment of my soul. We explored the Louvre and saw the Venus de Milo and Mona Lisa. She was not in any protection at all. No scarlet ropes separating her from the gallery, no glassed-in cover. Just there for all to see. We went to the Jeu de Plume where Monet's art was displayed all in one spot. His paintings were very large hanging practically from ceiling to floor. Impressionism remains my favorite. Later I traveled outside of Paris to Giverny where Monet's garden, Japanese bridge, and pond of lily pads was located. I ate in his garden, a Bibb lettuce salad with warm chicken livers with vinaigrette and a baguette. The living room of the farmhouse served as the elegant dining room. It was full because the French stop their business from noon until 2:00 for lunch, and it was now 1:00. They invited us, instead, to dine in the kitchen. The dining room table in the kitchen had chrome legs and was red but covered with a white linen tablecloth. There was silverware, white china with gold trim, linen napkins, and a flower in a bud vase on the table. We were the only ones there and were treaded like royalty.

In Paris, my brother and I went to the churches: Notre Dame built in 1163, Saint Chapelle built in 1245 to house the Crown of Thorns, both on the Ile de la Cite. We spent considerable time at Montmartre, an artist's gathering place with a funicular like Chateau Frontenac in Old Quebec, Canada. Montmartre is a large hill in the 18th arrondissement of the city. Its large white shimmering dome at the summit crowns the Basilica de la Sacre Coeur which overlooks the Right Bank and the night clubs. Artists that gather there. The 2004 movie *Moulin Rouge*, starring Nicole Kidman, is an accurate portrayal of the nightclub, the neighborhood, and Paris. In the movie, you see Toulouse Lautrec, which is accurate. He was the famous artist who drew the entertainers of the club. Notre Dame was badly damaged by fire in 2019. The Rose Window was saved. It was dirty but unharmed by the fire. Both its neighbor, Saint Chapelle and Notre Dame, are continuing sources of history about the beginnings of Paris. Also, on the Ile de la Cite is located the Conciergerie Prison where Marie Antoinette was held awaiting beheading in 1793. There is a more contemporary memorial on the island, the Memorial des Martyr's de la Deportation, to remember the 200,000 French citizens who were deported to German labor camps during WWII. The Ile de la Cite is the center of French measurement. 0km is located at the square of Place du Parvis de Notre Dame facing the two western towers of the church. It is the heart of Paris and the point from which all French mileage is determined.

Stevie and I explored, and we did so all in French. Both of us were fluent. We became tour guides for the rest of the family especially when my grandparents arrived. Grandfather and Grandmother Fee, my mother's parents, came to be part of our summer family European Grand Tour.

We were part of European tradition dating back to 1800s France and England wherein couples of means would visit France, Germany, Italy, and Spain on their honeymoon, a honeymoon that lasted for months or years. Henry James, an English novelist of the 19th century wrote of their adventures. Now we would have our own adventures.

We all gathered in Saint Germain-en- Laye where we had moved to between my freshman and sophomore years. Saint Germain was the birthplace of Louis XIV where his father, Louis XIII had a chateau with walls, turrets, stables, and a formal inner court garden. My very last day in France was spent in that garden.

As Louis XIV grew up, he learned to hunt in the Royal Wood, which extended from Saint Germain-en-Laye to a small hunting lodge called Versailles. The Royal Wood was unpopulated except for the royal groundskeepers who made sure there was no poaching of game and kept the Wood replenished with deer and boar. The death penalty was the sentence for poachers. Daily there were hunting parties through the Wood and in time, as Louis grew, his heart changed from Saint Germain-en-Laye to Versailles, and he began the construction of the most famous palace in the world at the hunting lodge called Versailles.

Versailles, just outside of Paris as the Seine flows, was the de facto capital of France from 1682-1789 when Louis XVI was executed. His grandfather, Louis XIV was the mind, imagination, and power behind the building of the Palace. His paranoia of his own people overthrowing him kept a policy of French nobles living at Versailles for the entire length of royalty power. Only the French Revolution ended Versailles being the de facto capital for all time.

In the meantime, Saint Germain-en-Laye was used as a second hunting home and then after the Glorious Revolution in England, the home of exiled James II of England and VII of Scotland lived there, raised a family and died and was buried in 1701.

It is the birthplace of many famous persons including Louis XIV the Sun King, Louisa Maria Teresa Stuart 1692, known as the Princess Royal by the Jacobite's of Scotland, and Claude Debussy 1862. It was the center of the German occupation Army in WWII. Napoleon I located his cavalry in Saint Germain-en-Laye. There is a 1.5-mile terrace at the old Chateau from which you can view the Royal Wood, the Seine, and Paris. It is located 11.9 miles from Paris city center.

Supreme Headquarters Allied Powers Europe S.H.A.P.E. Village, a military housing complex, is located there. We moved in. It was a second-floor 4-bedroom apartment with a balcony. My grandparents arrived, and we gathered and planned about our trip and together left on our tour.

The Grand Tour

---------------------------------- ✑ ----------------------------------

W e drove to Germany. Our vehicle was a 1957 pink Bel Air Chevy station wagon complete with fins. It was always a crowd-maker as the Europeans are used to small compact cars and this was the opposite. It was also American. A rare sight at that time, 1960.

We drove through Germany, headed to the mountains to a recreational resort in the region called Garmisch. In the German region of Bavaria is found peoples who are very independent and conservative. In WWII, it was a stronghold for the Nazis. Hitler's Eagle's Lair is located here along with the towns of Munich, Nuremburg, and Dachau. The last two towns were part of Nazi extermination camps and Munich was a heavy manufacturing town, which was badly bombed during the War. Many years later, in 2020, Chancellor Angela Merkel thanked the Allies for liberation from Nazi rule on VE Day. She laid a wreath at Germany's Tomb of the Unknown Soldier in Berlin. She has been Chancellor since 2007. VE Day is May 8. She is one of my favorite politicians as she knows the cost of freedom; she is from East Berlin; she knows the Berlin Wall. She knows the price of freedom.

We saw the devastation of war as restoration was just getting underway. Garmisch was different. It was a beautiful, quaint village and the surrounding area was alps, lakes, flowering meadows, and resorts with toys for tourists to play with such as speed boats, horses, restaurants (I remember the oxtail soup), a bus line to get around, and access to a neighboring town called Oberammergau. The people of Bavaria are mostly Catholic and devout. In Oberammergau, there is a world-famous tradition of the reenactment of the Passion of Jesus Christ. I went to see this play with my brother, Stevie. It was very real. I forget how they got the actor playing Jesus to stay on the Cross, but he did. To be Jesus was the highest honor the town could bestow on a young man. The play comprised the 12 Stations of the Cross as depicted in Catholic tradition. It began with the arrest and trial of Jesus, continued through the scourging, and the carrying of the Cross with help from Simon, Veronica, and Mary, all of whom walked with Him on His painful journey. It ends with His death on the Cross. The Oberammergau Passion Play was extremely powerful. I remember crying. It has stayed with me over the years.

My brother and I also learned to water ski in a large lake at the bottom of a mountain in a valley. We took the rail to the summit of the Zugspitze and I still have the photo of him sitting atop the peak. It was summer so no snow or ice, just a spectacular view and tranquility. We went horseback riding, western saddle. I love to ride, mostly English saddle, but my brother was not as adventurous as I, so we went with western saddles. My mother and grandparents stayed close to the hotel, but we all went out at night to be a part of the entertainment. I remember my sister was chosen to play the xylophone along with the bandleader. At another evening, I was chosen to dance German folk dances with the men wearing Lederhosen. The women's German folk costume was beautiful and for sale all over the downtown dress shops. My brother bought Lederhosen and an alpine hat with pheasant feather. I still have these things. I put them in my hope chest where they are safely stored in a Maine mountain barn.

Our next stop was Italy. We were going to see Venice, Florence, Rome, and the Italian Alps. Monte Bianco or Mont Blanc is the highest peak in Western Europe, and it is here in this region. Our first stop was Rome. We saw all the main sights, but I remember most of all the food. Italian food is not like American Italian food. The ice cream stood out and then the pizza. Delicious.

In Paris, my art education had begun. Now we were at the Vatican and my bar for art appreciation became Michelangelo. I saw the Sistine Chapel, but what stands out in my memory is the Pieta. It was just beautiful. You could see her sorrow on her face. We went to the Coliseum but only saw the dungeons and the first floor. Today, all floors are open.

My father made sure we went to every museum and church to see what man could create and it has stayed with me. I have taught my family about museums and art galleries. We left my grandparents in Rome. They sailed back to New York on the way to Florida. We went on to Venice and Murano.

Murano was established in 1291 and has been the leader in glass works ever since. It is outside but nearby Rome. Venice is its neighbor. We parked our car in a multi-level parking garage in Murano, as one cannot take a vehicle to Venice. We stayed the night in Murano and explored the artists making blown glass into vases, sculpture, trinkets, glasses, and objects d'art. Dale Chihuly, the glass artist master who has exhibited in premier museums around Europe and America, is influenced by Murano. Chihuly's studio is in Washington State.

In the morning, the five of us got into a ferry and sailed to Venice, a short boat ride. I remember the pigeons in Saint Mark's Square. My outstanding memory of Venice was a gondola, wherein entering another gondola, was my acquaintance Kim. She was a striking blond from my school, though I did not speak to her, as she was an upperclassman. I called to her, but she did not hear, and I lost sight of her. Since Covid-19 the waters around Venice have cleared up and the dolphins and sea turtles and birds are returning. While we were there, crowds were in evidence but not overly so. Now it is a different story. The big cruise ships come, and the sightseers overpopulate the city. We saw the Church; we saw the bridges and the plaza. It had a great deal of atmosphere, but I was too young to appreciate the art of Venice. John Singer Sargent lived and painted there in the late 1800's. His works are at the Boston Museum of Fine Art and museums of quality throughout the world. He is considered the premier portrait painter of the Edwardian era. His oeuvre, Madame X, was intended to consolidate this position but resulted in scandal in society and the art world. He left Europe for England and then America. Mother was not feeling well, so my father put her on a train and sent her off to Paris. My mother was a delicate woman, and the long-distance driving was just too much for her. We took the ferry to Murano and retrieved the car and headed for Florence.

The four of us traveled north towards the Alps on our way to Florence. We stopped at a vineyard and met the grower and he offered us grapes from the vine to try. They were delicious and juicy. I had red juice dripping down my chin. Florence was a visual delight. It started by seeing the Medici Palace with the works of Michelangelo and led to the plaza that was home to David. It is perfect. Michelangelo would tell the story of sculptors saying there was an imperfection to David so he would take some marble dust in his hand without being seen and climb the ladder to the nose or part of the body the other sculptor mentioned, and he would pretend to chisel away and drop the dust. The complaining sculptor would think his correction was done and it was now perfect, yet Michelangelo never retouched the sculpture. David started to erode from the polluted air so he was moved indoors where he can still be seen. On the Ponte Vecchio is a bridge from centuries ago and on this bridge are jewelry stores. The finest craftsmanship can be found here. My father and I went to this bridge and he surprised me with a gold bangle bracelet. It was just a treasure. Many years later, I passed the bracelet on to my daughter, but it was stolen and is gone forever. Paris and Florence are my favorite European cities. They both left lasting impressions on me. We left Florence and drove back to Paris. We went to Spain at Easter. My brother was able to join us. We went to the Spanish Rivera outside of Barcelona. It was a bank holiday. Easter in Europe is a very big deal. We had no Spanish money so we could not conduct any business or eat at cafes. We had sardines, bread, and peanut butter. I grew to love sardines. After the holiday we went to cafes and shops. My father bought me a blue and white bathing suit. My brother and I went to the paddleboats and paddled to a US Navy destroyer anchored just offshore. My brother decided to ram the boat. He enjoyed himself immensely, but I was a wreck. The sailors on the bow of the ship laughed loudly. Together we watched Spanish folk dancing and joined in. The resort village we were in was very untouched by the tourists. Now that has changed. It was located just outside of Barcelona. Barcelona is the home of the sculptor Gaudi. Gaudi spent his life building the cathedral La Sagrada with unique architecture the likes of which I had never seen before. It is truly unique. It looks like it is from outer space. His materials for sculpting were limestone, cement or plaster, broken tile and pottery and colored glass. He made sculptures to sing with visual delight and wonder. He designed a park, Parc Guell, which is a complete park done in fanciful walkways, paths, benches, tiles, and pottery. Gaudi was an original and he devoted his artistic life to Barcelona. His buildings and his park are memorable and unique. After Barcelona, we drove to Paris where we remained except for two side-trips, which did not include my brother as he went back to school.

In my sophomore year in the fall, my mother and I went to East Berlin on a military troop transport train. We were in the private car and we travelled through Russian-German zones and American-German zones. This was before the Berlin Wall went up. It was 1960. President Kennedy was still in office.

East Berlin

There are three events that shaped my adult life. They all happened in the 60s in a span of seven years: The first was my visit to Berlin. This visit opened my eyes to the devastation and pain of war, dictatorship, and the necessity of war in extreme times such as Hitler. The second was my marriage, which gave me my children and the State of Maine. My marriage produced the children of my heart and the knowledge that finally I had a hometown. The third was the death of my brother in service to his country. In Berlin, I had seen the price of war, and in my brother's sacrifice to his country, the price of freedom. Over the years, I have learned that many do not understand freedom, nor do they even know what Gold Star Family, sister, widow, widower, brother means. I have had to explain it many times. There is little respect.

Gold Star Family means that a loved partner or sibling was killed in Action in Service to his or her country. Many do not know this or what the initials GS stand for. President Trump does not know what Gold Star means as he called, in a press conference, those who have sacrificed their life for the common good of the country losers. Those who have given lovingly and proudly to our country are not losers: they are our heroes and the guardians of our country's very soul. We must protect their memories from this assault on their sacrifice. Heroes come in different shapes and sizes, colors and races. The lone black Capitol Policeman who led the Epiphany Capitol Insurrection insurrectionists away from the House chamber where a joint session of Congress was deliberating is a living hero. He was almost a dead one. The historic date is January 6, 2021. Amen.

When we arrived in West Berlin, we went to the Tempelhof Airport Hotel, which was to be our residence while in Berlin and was ground zero for the Berlin Airlift immediately following WWII. At the end of WWII, Berlin was divided into 4 Sectors: American, French, British, Russian. The Russians were not happy with this division and so cut off Berlin from the world using its infrastructure against them. The people began to starve, medical supplies were non-existent, and the children had nothing. The situation was dire when Lieutenant Gail Halvorsen newly stationed at Tempelhof Airfield in Berlin became aware of the plight of the children. They had nothing, and a part of a piece of gum or just sniffing a gum wrapper gave them delight. Lt. Halvorsen said he would drop some candy over the city. The children asked how they would know it was him and he said he would wiggle his wings. He became known the Candy Bomber or Uncle Wiggly Wings. After a short time, this became a national effort and by the end of Operation Little Vittles, the pilots had dropped 23 tons of candy along with 250,000 parachutes used to drop the candy gently to ground. Operation Little Vittles ran from September 22, 1948-May 13, 1949. It was an American success in spreading goodwill. Among the many medals and citations given to Colonel Halvorsen is the Medal for Humanity and the German medal Order of Merit.

My mother and I arrived in American Sector Berlin in the spring of 1960. West Berlin was thriving. The streets were lined with busy, brightly dressed, happy people. The trees were blooming and lined the streets. There were tulips in bloom and spring flowers were starting to show their beautiful colors. The double-decker buses were crowded and music and laughter could be heard. We went to the three sectors, and they were all having the same atmosphere: the "I made it" breath of new life as coming out of death. There were shops and sidewalk cafés. It was bustling. I would say the French, British, and American Sectors were the color of bright sunshine yellow. The color of the Russian Sector was grey.

Russian troops lined the Brandenburg Gate, the entryway to East Berlin. Freedom stopped at the gate. I spoke to the soldiers in German, they responded in Russian. No one knew what was being said but they were smiling. They were not much older than me. The thoroughfare was named Lenin Strasse. It was as though the sun went away. It all seemed shrouded in fog. There were no trees or flowers. The atmosphere was very heavy.

My mother and I boarded a tour bus. I had the window seat so I could see very well. I looked with an intensity that produced years later, a clear memory of oppression. We drove the Sector length of Lenin Strasse, which was about 1 ½ miles long. The main street was 4-lanes with sidewalks and modern square shaped buildings. It was all the same color, concrete grey. The first floors had large panes of glass and the upper floors a series of small rectangular windows. There was no imagination in the designs. The buildings had spaces between them, spaces with no vegetation or sidewalks. Just spaces. Behind the spaces, you could see the rubble of war.

The view was about two blocks deep from the street. It was all bombed out buildings and bare tree trunk stumps. It was piles of bombed buildings, piles of dust. The only color was shades of grey. The movies of The Battle of the Bulge show bombed out empty expanses where once there had been pasture, wood, villages…well, this view of war was just like them. It remains a daytime nightmare.

As we slowly drove the length of downtown, one could not help but begin to compare East and West Berlin. In the West, there was beauty, there was color, there were people, and there was life. In the East, it was the opposite. In the East, there was death. While I was looking out the window a pedestrian came into view. I focused on her. She was coming toward me, so I got a good look. She was the only person I saw the entire afternoon that I was in East Berlin. She was slender, wearing an overcoat and on her head, a babushka. She was carrying a shopping bag and a purse. Her head was bowed, looking at the ground as she shuffled down the street. Her clothes were grey. She seemed as though she were sad. We drove by her, leaving me to sort out this new impression. We drove on to the Soviet War Memorial.

The van took a right, and we turned onto a side street. This street took us to a park. In Western Europe, parks are central in location and easily accessed. In East Berlin, the park was practically hidden. We came to the parking area and I saw a lawn leading to a huge concrete statue. This was the first thing I saw in East Berlin that had color. There were flowers lining a walkway to the statue and the statue, a tribute to Soviet dead, was tall, square, and massive. This type of sculpture is found all over Russian or Soviet cities and territories. In Central Asia, they prevail. In Iceland, the sculpture is similar but mostly about Vikings or Viking things. We stayed in the park a short while. Most war memorials have a sense of spirituality about them. The Soviet one spoke none of that. It was just a huge block with Russian words on it. When we were done, we headed back to the Brandenburg Gate. I reflected that I had just seen what happens when the Cold War escalates.

I was born in war and raised in the Cold War, a war that for most is just a footnote in a history book. Starting in New Mexico, we were stationed at these sensitive areas of the country, learning how to win the Cold War or fight it. Alabama was the home of the Army War College and Korea was the Cold War gone hot. After his bombing missions in Germany ended, my father was placed with intelligence. He was number two in Paris at S.H.A.P.E. He was responsible for the war games played with our NATO allies. Our final deployment was at Wright-Patterson Air Force Base where he was Commander of Foreign Intelligence Division.

He never ever talked about his work or his bombing missions, but he did talk about jets and Korea. I think his greatest thrill was in his attempt to break the sound barrier and his happiest time was in retirement as he pursued his passion for rocks and then gems and then jewelry stores.

The Cold War goes on. There have been changes in the direction of the war. The Russians were so keen on keeping people in their territories they tried to kill them if they escaped. They even built a wall. Thanks to President Reagan, the Berlin Wall came down. We thought the war was over, but recently Russia stole our intelligence, our nuclear codes, and did severe damage to our technical apparatus, so the war goes on, the rules have just been changed.

We drove back through the Brandenburg Gate and entered the American Sector Berlin. What a relief. I was getting very fond of President Kennedy. He asked, "What can you do for your Country? Not, what can your Country do for you?" He and his wife, Jackie, conquered Europe, and he was the very embodiment of freedom. The good ones get assassinated. I went to his funeral. I was in downtown

DC and the procession came right by me. I was standing on a corner of a street and no one was in front of me. You could hear a pin drop, it was so eerily silent. The clopping of the horses was the only sound. It was sad. I will never forget it. The sadness of the country was palpable on the street in Washington, DC. Stevie is buried a block from the President's grave. I go to both frequently. The gravesite visits do not quell my sadness as there was a vacuum created when the President was shot and killed and then, when my brother was shot and killed, both in the head. Dreams died, families ended, government changed, and we had to start over.

My mother and I went to the Tempelhof Airport Hotel, boarded a train and returned to Paris. We had a side trip in France to take. Summer was coming. My brother would be home.

The French Riviera

———————— ❦ ————————

After our return from Berlin, it was back to school and waiting for Stevie to arrive in Paris. He did so at the end of May, arriving on a Military Air Transport plane from New York. The upcoming year would be his last at Saint Paul's Preparatory School in Concord, New Hampshire. During the school year, he spent holidays with his cousins the Waller's who lived in Cheshire, Connecticut. It was a convenient and happy arrangement, as the Waller's had three boys just a bit shy of Stevie's age. Their mother, Marjorie Jane, was our mother's older sister. My mother and Aunt Marj were the best of friends and stayed very close until Aunt Marj's death in 1992. My mother died in 1995. Both sisters died in South Florida where they had retired. They liked to travel on the Queen Elizabeth II going on world tours and Mediterranean cruises. These cruises kept the two sisters lively and funny. My mother wrote poetry about her experiences on the ship and her opus, *Life's Great on the Queen,* is a treasured keepsake and memory. I had just turned 15.

Upon his arrival in France, Stevie spent a few days with us in St Germain-en-Laye and then met up with his classmate, John Kerry

'65, for a biking tour of the Atlantic coasts of Brittany and Normandy, which were regions of France across from the English Channel and the island of Great Britain. John Kerry's grandmother lived in a chateau on the coast of Brittany, which is why Secretary Kerry speaks French fluently. He went on to become the 68th Secretary of State from 2013-2017. He was defeated in his Presidential bid by incumbent George Bush.

Stevie and John biked all through the two regions and stopped to visit friends along the way. They finished their tour in Paris staying on the Ile Saint Louis. I do believe this trip was a highlight of my brother's life, and the two were friends even beyond death, as Senator Kerry had lunch with my oldest son, Christos III, in the Senate Dining Room at a table with three chairs, one being empty for Stevie.

When the biking tour was over, Stevie rejoined the family, and we left for the French Riviera. It was the beginning of July and perfect weather awaited us on the coast of the Mediterranean. We drove in the pink Chevy station wagon and arrived in Cannes during the height of the tourist season. What struck me was the Promenade de la Croisette, a road and walkway that went for 2km between the beach and the hotels and casinos. The hotels were of the highest quality set back from the promenade with spaces of gardens, palm trees, and walkways leading to the grand entrances. We were on the dining terrace of one having lunch, and I distinctly remember a fellow patron ordering and eating Steak Tartare. Now, this particular dish is raw with spices, and I was just fascinated with his meal. It did not seem to make him ill. I, myself, would never try it.

At 1 Promenade de la Croisette is the Palais des Festivals et des Congres. This large structure is a convention center where the Cannes Film Festival is held. It is very grand and luxurious. I did not see it, as it was not built until 1982. While we were in Cannes, in 1960, the American tourist was just beginning to flock there, it was mostly British tourists at that time. Along the Promenade were chic, expensive boutiques and restaurants with grand terraces, which were dining areas, so you could look out over the Cote D'Azure and hotels. The beach had lots of white rocks and then sand. The water was temperate with softly rolling waves breaking on the shore. The sea near the coast was full of yachts and ships. There were lots of sunbrellas on the beach with many sunbathing guests. It was crowded and looked like a great deal of fun. We did not stay long, just walking the length of the Promenade to take everything in. The next day, we went to St. Tropez driving the road called the Esterel Corniche following the Golfe de St. Tropez.

The Esterel Corniche is a narrow, winding coastal road with the cliffs of France coming down to the gulf with a level two-lane country road leveled out of them. It is very beautiful, but one must be aware and pay close attention to the curves. There is no shoulder. The road empties at the mouth of the gulf, which is town center for St. Tropez. Out in Golfe de St. Tropez can be seen yachts from all over the world, and they were of all sizes and beauty. The town center is horseshoe shaped with the center being level and crowded with restaurants and sidewalk cafes, a flower market, and a food market. The mouth of the Golfe St. Tropez begins here. Beyond the levelness of the center are the cliffs going practically straight up. It is in this area that the villas and homes are located but it is not large. Bridgette Bardot lives here quietly with her dogs that she rescued and cares for. She remains a French icon.

In the town proper we went to a restaurant and sat outside, under a canopy overlooking the Golfe St. Tropez. What I noticed in the French restaurants is that the food is very fresh. To be sure it is fresh, the proprietors have fish aquariums in a highly visible section of the dining room. Large Mediterranean and Atlantic fish are swimming around in these tanks, and if you wish to eat fish for your déjeuner, you pick one out. The waiter retrieves it out of the tank and next thing you know, you are eating it. It is all quite adventurous. The waiter takes the head and tail off and takes the bone out. As I clearly recall, it was a bit macabre but delicious.

We stayed in St. Tropez three-quarters of the day and then drove on to Carcassonne where we spent the night and next day. At that instant I did not know that Carcassonne would become part of my brother's and my life. It seems that we are related to King Henry II.

1158AD. King Henry II, King of England, Wales, Scotland, Ireland, Brittany, Normandy, and Aquitaine had just lost his successor. He ruled like all Norman kings, in Carcassonne. This city is now part of our heritage. His oldest son, Henry, had died and the next in line was a fool named John. That left Richard and Jeffry. Their mother, Eleanor of Aquitaine, a 6-foot-tall fiery redhead was in the mix also. Christmas Eve and the King imprisons his sons and his wife. King Henry brings in his mistress whom he loves, Alice. All this and the family are in the dungeon. A big sword fight happens and who will be the successor is settled. It is a very dysfunctional family dynamic with an empire at stake. As it turns out, Henry dies a natural death a short time later and the fool John became king. Under his reign, the empire weakened and crumbled. He died and Richard took over. Under his reign, the United Kingdom and Southwestern France flourished. He became known as Richard the Lionhearted. Henry II, John, and Richard never lived in England. They lived and operated out of Carcassonne. However, Richard is buried on the island. My brother is a direct line to King Henry II through the King's mistress, Ada. We link our line to Audrey Barlowe, my 8th great grandmother. Her son was Christopher Almy. His daughter

Elizabeth Almy was the grandmother of Lewis Morris, Signer of the Declaration of Independence. Their grandson was Charles Augustus Morris, the father of my great-grandmother Nettie Morris Tracy.

But back in the 1100s, French King Louis IX began to fortify Carcassonne and his son, Philip III, continued the work. Carcassonne was and is a walled fortified medieval city. It is a sight to behold and upon entering, Stevie and I ran the ramparts, shot arrows through the wall's slits, and played at jousting though there were no horses. The city is settled on the Aube River near the coast, but you cannot see the coast, and a plain surrounds Carcassonne. Nearby, coincidently, is Beziers where I went with the Religious of the Sacred Heart of Mary and had a thoroughly fascinating stay during a convocation while I was a student at Marymount-sur-seine a Neuilly in Paris. This area of France is very precious to me. After our exploration of Carcassonne, we drove back to Paris and spent the remainder of the summer at our home in Saint Germain-en-Laye.

Saint Germain-en-Laye and Ohio

— ❦ —

When we moved from the Parisienne suburb of Le Vesinet, we moved to the historic home of King Louis XIII. Prince Louis XIV, who became known as the Sun King, was born at this chateau central to the new city we had relocated to. Saint Germain was a typical French residential town with an outdoor food market in the center of town, a heavily used train station from out of Gard du Nord, a taxi stand, boutiques such as Cartier and Gucci, and the Chateau. My last day in France was spent in the manicured French garden of Chateau Saint Germain.

Saint Germain was founded in 1020 when King Robert the Pious built a convent on the site of the present-day Church of Saint Germain. The region was part of the lush European forest and rich in venison and wild boar, perfect for royalty. The many kings who lived here had peasants called gamekeepers patrolling the forest for poachers as no one could hunt the Royal Wood but the king and his hunting party. The party went out almost daily. The hunt was exercise, camaraderie, food, exploration, entertainment, stature, and more. It was the center of chateau life. Poachers would be killed. About 2 hours away through the forest, King Louis XIII discovered the hunting lodge at Versailles. He loved the location so very much that he began to build a chateau. It was his son, Louis XIV the Sun King, that made the palace so grand. Louis XIV loved Versailles so much he moved his government out of Paris to Versailles and it was not until the French Revolution that French government returned to Paris. Louis XVI lost his head over the splendor and expense of maintaining the gardens and the buildings.

Louis XIV moved to Versailles during the time of The Glorious Revolution, the war between England and Scotland. King James of Scotland lost his throne and his land, there was a price on his head, and he went into exile living at the Chateau of Saint Germain-en-Laye. King James's daughter, Louisa Maria Stuart, was born here in 1692. King James died and was buried here. He never returned to Scotland or England.

Following WWI, the Treaty of Saint Germain was signed here marking the end of the Hapsburg dynasty and freedom for Poland, Czechoslovakia, Hungary, and the Croatia and Serbian regions. The end of WWII was signed at Versailles. During this war, Saint Germain-en-Laye was the headquarters of the German Army. Napoleon I had located his headquarters for his Calvary campaigns here. Saint Germain is central to French military campaigns and history. We were smack in the middle of it all.

Supreme Headquarters Allied Powers Europe S.H.A.P.E. Village was just outside of town center. It is a military apartment complex for the officers and non-coms who worked for the NATO complex. The complex was built in a cow pasture. I memorized the Shakespeare play *Romeo and Juliette* sitting with the cows. They were dairy cows. The apartment buildings were 3 stories high. There was a small chateau for use as a social center and it held many different group activities. I remember I taught catechism in that chateau to elementary school children. There were teen dances. For the different schools, the chateau was the pickup and drop off place for the students from all our Allied friends. In my building, there were American, British, and Canadian families. My best friend was a German girl named Barbara. Her father was a German Air Force Colonel. He had lost half a leg in a POW camp. I heard, years later, that he had been tried as an East German spy and was executed. War is tragic, hot or cold. Sometimes I skipped school to go to Paris, I figured that would be more of an education. I knew my way around like a Parisienne and my French accent was perfect. I have lost the accent since. My brother spoke French like a Frenchman or so the citizens of France told him. He was very proud of his linguistics abilities; he spoke German, Latin, Greek, as well as French. If you know Latin, you can learn any language easily. The life in France was in the era of bobby socks and saddle shoes, crew cuts, and skinny ties. It was a time of revelation about the world and the time came to an end.

We were to relocate to Ohio. We could have extended our tour for another year, but Stevie was graduating from school and this was a very big deal. He was going to Princeton University '65. I still had two years left so we flew to New York. We drove to Concord, New Hampshire, for the graduation ceremony. Stevie won the linguistics prize for the entire class of '61 and the prize was an exquisite set of red leather-bound French books by the philosophers/writers of the Enlightenment movement including John Locke, Voltaire, Jean Jacques Rousseau, and Renee Descartes. The Enlightenment, late 17th and early 18th centuries, was a time of intellectual expansion and experiment stressing individualism and reason rather than tradition.

Our own Benjamin Franklin was quite attracted to this movement. He was a beloved hero and darling of the French Court and the ladies of the Parisienne salons. The French Award Books rest in Saint Paul's Preparatory School library. They are safe there. I believe the Enlightenment Period was partially responsible for the French Revolution.

Following the senior year graduation, we drove to Dayton, Ohio. The Chevy pink station wagon was left behind and we rented a sedan to make the drive. We drove straight through and reached Ohio in good time. We went straight to Wright-Patterson Air Force Base located outside of Dayton in a community called Fairborn. The base was very secure and to get past the guards at the gates you had to prove who you were. We moved into a Tudor style two-story home near the Officer's Club and golf course. There was also an inside swimming pool where I swam a mile several days a week and an outdoor swimming social center. It had high diving boards of all heights and a couple of kiddie pools. Stevie played golf with Mom and in the winter, we iced skated nearby at a skating pond.

We spent the summer exploring the region around us. This included the Indian Snake Mounds and Antioch College. To say I was suffering from a severe case of culture shock is an understatement. For the first time in our moves around the country I was having a hard time. It took two years to acclimate to the USA. Stevie had friends from Saint Paul and Princeton who lived in the area. I think he spent time in Cincinnati and Columbus. We knew this would be our last station, so we luxuriated in it. I went to school in Dayton, a private girl's school, and Steve left for New Jersey and Princeton. At school, I learned about the Cinderella Modeling School in Dayton so enrolled and ended up working there as a receptionist. Before I would go to work, I would have a bowl of chili at Rike's Department Store.

It was a ritual. Stevie did not have the problem of being the new kid in class, but I did. It was difficult for me but a breeze for my brother.

When he arrived at Princeton, Stevie had friends already and made new ones with his dorm partners and his study group. His dorm was rooms in an apartment with three other students. They even had a kitchen and a living room. It was all quite lovely. He joined the Princeton University's Colonial Club, something of a fraternity. He remains a member. I went to Princeton twice. Once while in Dayton and once while at Marymount University of Virginia. I was obviously not Ivy League as my brother was, so I did not really fit in with his lifestyle. We would spend the two summers we had at Wright-Patterson Air Force Base with the other military children on the base and with some people at the University of Dayton. Stevie spent quite a bit of time with Mother who was going through her own culture shock. They played golf frequently, and I remember Sundays at the Officer's Club after church for brunch. The church was on the base. It even had its own dry cleaner. I learned to drive here. My father, a jet pilot taught me. I became an excellent driver and student.

My first flight experience was here. I flew in a Link Trainer, which is a flight simulator. I was told I flew through a mountaintop and landed under the ground, so I did not do well at that time. Later this would be much different. My brother had always wanted to be a pilot, but he found out that he got airsick. This was a major disappoint to him. He remembered that he loved to surf, and he had a great love for the ocean. He wished, upon completion of college to go to graduate school for Oceanography. This was not to happen, as Vietnam was becoming a huge problem for the current administration and the new war, which was never declared a war, but a conflict would devour the country while he was in school. From here, events are jumbled, as there was so very much turmoil in the country.

Stevie had been raised in a soldier's way with discipline, focus, and strategy, so he completed school with the focus on surviving the conflict. He knew he had a destiny to fulfill. For his graduation gift he went back to France. It was the highlight of his life. When he returned from France, he began to teach in Florida at a local elementary school biding his time until he knew if his life would be civilian or military. President Johnson decided for him in the form of the draft. He chose to be a Marine, the best of the best. It would be infantry and translator. He went to Monterey, California, to Defense Language School and turned his ease of languages into fluency of Vietnamese. In Officer's Candidacy School, he graduated second in his class with his competition saying he was always so close to being number one, but his competitor was just a touch fiercer.

During this time of transition from peace to war, I graduated high school and entered college. Marymount, the first school I really enjoyed was to be this college. I signed on for two years. To start this new life, I went from Dayton, Ohio, to Arlington, Virginia, and discovered that the metro area of DC was very familiar to me, and I felt I had come home. I never saw Dayton again. It was, in the summer of 1963, that finding myself in DC, I attended the "I Have a Dream" speech. I will never forget it. There were so many people of color on the Mall to hear the speech that I knew it would become a moment in time of greatness. Martin Luther King spoke, but Mahalia Jackson sang out, "Preach it, Pastor, Preach it," and he did with his words ringing over the Mall. There was only the sound of the Reverend preaching equality and peaceful protest, words true today. People were attentive and soaking in The Reverend's "I Have a Dream" speech. They were dressed in their Sunday best. There was a smattering of white people and they too listened attentively. I was in Washington, DC, to await the opening of my college and walked over from where I had been staying near Rock Creek Parkway.

During my freshman year, Stevie's third, my father retired and moved the family back to Lake Worth, Florida. I was coming out of culture shock and the nuns were sympathetic to my dilemma. I adjusted to life as a civilian and a Floridian living in Washington. I did not go to Florida very often; I stayed on at school. At a school mixer with Georgetown University, I met my husband to be. He was from Maine, the first I had heard of New England. I knew my relatives in Connecticut and had been to Concord, New Hampshire, but I had never heard the term New England, and it was all quite romantic. He swept me off my feet. I think I had made an unconscious decision to live life as a civilian. I really longed for permanency. I avoided military academy students but went to President Johnson's Inauguration Ball with an Air Force cadet. No, I wanted permanency.

Stevie entered the USMC and married his high school sweetheart. His life was before him, but the times were against him. Vietnam was very difficult. As a young man of the right age, your chances of avoiding military service were nil. He died in a rice paddy on June 2, 1967. He was a hero. To me, he will always be a surfer, he will forever be a Spirit of the Sea.

The Cherry Bomb Caper

It was summer 1964. It was hot. The base young men had been entertaining the base young ladies at the pool all summer, but this day was different. The Air Force Cadets had arrived. The entire sophomore class of cadets was on base tour to find wives. The cadets traveled to each major Air Force Base for tours and orientations and girls. Today they were here. The base young men were not happy.

After several days and evenings of the cadets taking over the female population of the base, the young men came together in a summit and planned to avenge themselves. Of the young men in this group were the leader, Wood R., and my brother, Steve K., number one and two on the base as their fathers were the number one and two in command.

The fifties and early 60's were a time of cap pistols, firecrackers, sparklers, and the famous cherry bomb. Young boys played cowboys and Indians, pirates and Army with plenty of television role models like the Lone Ranger and Tonto, Peter Pan and Captain Hook, Sky King, Davy Crockett, and their fathers who were all military. Stevie was a leader among his peers and a good shot, so he was usually victorious in his play battles and learned about strategy and leadership and the use of the explosive in the form of a cherry bomb. He was partial to the cherry bomb.

When we lived in Florida and visited Sanibel Island before it was discovered, he would take cherry bombs and throw them in the surf to watch the water and fish fly up in a crescendo of sand and water. He got a thrill from this. He blew up anthills also and tonight, in Ohio, he and his men would ambush the cadets late at night while they were in their barracks.

The dark night was well into the early hours when, at 0200 hours, the Base Raiders struck. The raiders drove to the cadets barracks located in a remote part of the air base in the woods. They parked away from the one-story structure. It was built like an Indian longhouse. The raiders had selected a heavily wooded and secluded corner of the barracks wherein to attack. They dug a one-foot-deep trench on the two sides of the chosen corner. There was no sound.

The Base Raiders dropped 6 cherry bombs in the trench, setting the cherry bombs on fire. The raiders ran for cover in the woods, the cherry bombs went off and a loud explosion was heard and the cadets, already skilled in military training came running from all directions. The barracks had a small fire.

The cadets, awakened from deep sleep quickly regained alertness, threw anything they could find on, and met outside by the front door. Quickly a search party was ordered, and these seekers ran for the damaged corner of the building. They disappeared into the wood.

By the time the cadets found the raiders parking area, the raiders were long gone. The officer in charge of the cadets called the Military Police (MPs). An All-Points Bulletin (APB) was put out on the perpetrators. The perpetrators vanished.

The General-in-Command, of whom his son was the ringleader, was called and notified. The General told the MPs to call the Second-in-Command, of whom his son was number two of the Raiders and the MPs were given some clues. With those clues the MPs, young men themselves, put the whole night together and detained the raiders, my brother included. A reprimand was given, all was forgiven, and it became legend.

The Spider Web

B irch, my youngest grandson, had just put in his order for white and grey yarn with which to make spider webs when his order reminded me of Stevie's Spider Webs.

He would pick an enclosed room with one door like bathrooms, closets, small bedrooms, and studies. Starting at the back wall and as high as his head he would begin to weave the white twine from top to bottom. He made the rows of the web so tight you could not penetrate the web. He would weave the string back and forth, up and down, under and over until he got to the door while walking backwards.

Stevie would work so quietly and quickly that it was done and set before anyone else knew what he was up to. Then, he would lie in wait for someone to try and enter. As the person struggled more and more, he would show himself laughing. He was a big prankster. I was usually his target because I was his younger sister.

One web I remember was the bathroom in Falls Church, Virginia, where we were living in an old two-story home. The family was moving to Lake Barcroft, also in Virginia, so the Falls Church home was all packed up. It was Stevie's hope that the new tenant would need this room and would be unable to access it.

But I needed this one room and quick. It was an emergency. I started to pull on the web, to pull it down, to pull it apart. The web was holding. The harder I tried to part the web, the harder it became. I was frantic. But, just in the knick of time, my big brother appeared, and in his hand were scissors. He had his joke. Laughing the whole time. Just in time. He was always just in time nearby guarding.

When we were little and playing together, he would often just stop play and lean over and hug me and kiss me on the forehead. When we were teenagers, we went to the television studio inside the DC hotel to tape the Milt Grant Record Hop. He would dance only with me. He led us near the cameras and held me just right. He protected me from the dark forces at night. He was my hero. He was my brother.

A Gift from France

Beurre Blanc

6 cup saucepan
2 ½ tablespoons white wine vinegar
2 ½ tablespoons dry white wine
1 tablespoon minced shallots
½ tsp sal1/8 teaspoon white pepper
2 tablespoons butter
Combine and reduce
Add 2 sticks butter
Maybe lemon juice*

The sauce as it melts the sticks of melted butter should be thick and cream in color.

Pour on fish, vegetables, and mashed potatoes.

A French favorite

Bibliography

Child, Julia, et al. *Mastering the Art of French Cooking*. Alfred A. Knopf, 2009.

Photo Permission

NSDAR Convention Photo, 2017, Constitution Hall, Washington DC, Convention Photography.

CPSIA information can be obtained
at www.ICGtesting.com
Printed in the USA
LVHW041750100222
710655LV00002B/289

9 781665 540407